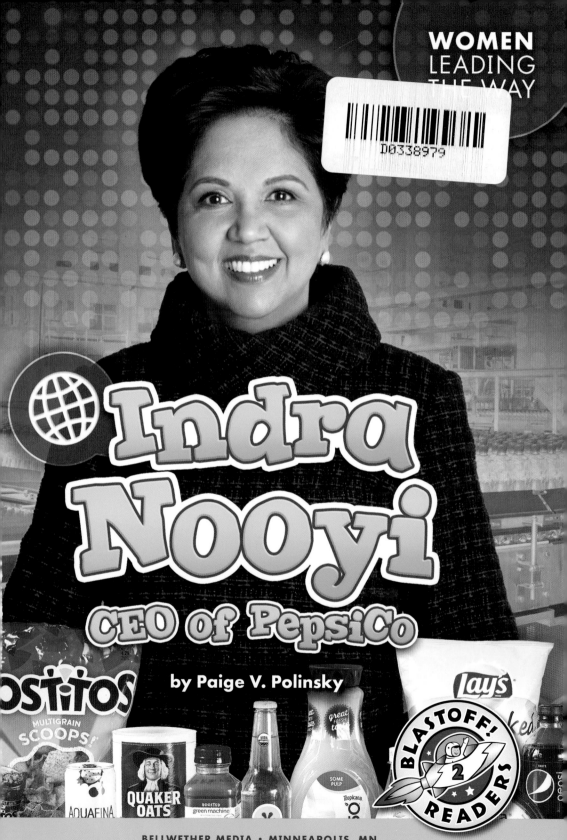

D0338979

Indra Nooyi
CEO of PepsiCo

by Paige V. Polinsky

BLASTOFF!
2
READERS

BELLWETHER MEDIA • MINNEAPOLIS, MN

Note to Librarians, Teachers, and Parents:

Blastoff! Readers are carefully developed by literacy experts and combine standards-based content with developmentally appropriate text.

Level 1 provides the most support through repetition of high-frequency words, light text, predictable sentence patterns, and strong visual support.

Level 2 offers early readers a bit more challenge through varied simple sentences, increased text load, and less repetition of high-frequency words.

Level 3 advances early-fluent readers toward fluency through increased text and concept load, less reliance on visuals, longer sentences, and more literary language.

Level 4 builds reading stamina by providing more text per page, increased use of punctuation, greater variation in sentence patterns, and increasingly challenging vocabulary.

Level 5 encourages children to move from "learning to read" to "reading to learn" by providing even more text, varied writing styles, and less familiar topics.

Whichever book is right for your reader, Blastoff! Readers are the perfect books to build confidence and encourage a love of reading that will last a lifetime!

This edition first published in 2019 by Bellwether Media, Inc.

No part of this publication may be reproduced in whole or in part without written permission of the publisher. For information regarding permission, write to Bellwether Media, Inc., Attention: Permissions Department, 6012 Blue Circle Drive, Minnetonka, MN 55343.

Library of Congress Cataloging-in-Publication Data

LC record for Indra Nooyi: CEO of PepsiCo available at https://lccn.loc.gov/2018033435

Editor: Kate Moening   Designer: Andrea Schneider

Printed in the United States of America, North Mankato, MN.

Table of Contents

Who Is Indra Nooyi?

Indra Nooyi is the first woman to lead PepsiCo. She was **CEO** for 12 years.

PepsiCo is one of the biggest **companies** in the world!

PepsiCo headquarters

"WHATEVER YOU DO, THROW YOURSELF INTO IT. THROW YOUR HEAD, HEART, AND HANDS INTO IT." (2007)

Getting Her Start

Indra was born in India. She grew up there with her sister, Chandrika.

Their mom taught them to dream big.

New York,
United States
PepsiCo headquarters

Madras (Chennai), India
Indra's birthplace

Young Indra played **cricket** and climbed trees. She was in a rock band.

Indra Nooyi Profile

Birthday: October 28, 1955

Hometown: Madras, India
(now known as Chennai, India)

Industry: business

Education:
- chemistry degree
  (Madras Christian College)
- business degree
  (Indian Institute of Management)
- management degree (Yale University)

Influences and Heroes:
- Shantha Krishnamurthy (mother)
- Roger Enrico (former PepsiCo CEO)
- Steve Reinemund
  (former PepsiCo CEO)
- Steve Jobs (former CEO of Apple, Inc.)

Indra worked hard in school.
She studied science and **business**.

Indra finished college early. Her mother wanted her to get married.

Indra moved to the United States instead. She studied business in Connecticut.

Yale School of Management

Changing the World

Indra worked with many companies. She planned ways for them to grow.

PepsiCo **hired** Indra in 1994. She made its **products** look better.

In 2006, Indra became PepsiCo's CEO. She decided to make PepsiCo products healthier.

Many people said this would fail. But **consumers** loved it!

"BRING TOGETHER WHAT IS GOOD FOR BUSINESS WITH **WHAT IS GOOD FOR THE WORLD.**" (2013)

Indra was very busy.
Family members helped
Indra and her husband
raise their two daughters.

Sometimes Indra felt like a bad mom. But she fought hard to build her **career**.

In 2018, Indra said she was leaving PepsiCo.

Indra Nooyi Timeline

1978   Indra graduates from the Indian Institute of Management and moves to the United States

1994   Indra starts working at PepsiCo

2006   Indra becomes CEO of PepsiCo

2010   *Fortune* magazine names Indra 'Most Powerful Woman in Business' for the fifth year in a row

2018   Indra announces she is leaving PepsiCo

NEW YORK STOCK EXCHANGE

She made important changes in the company. Her changes are helping people make healthier choices.

Indra wants to see more women build careers in business.

There are few women CEOs today. But Indra Nooyi is leading the way!

"REMAIN A LIFELONG STUDENT. **DON'T LOSE THAT CURIOSITY.**" (2013)

Glossary

business—the act of making, buying, or selling goods for money

career—a job that someone does for a long time

CEO—the highest-ranking person in a company; CEO stands for "chief executive officer."

companies—groups that make, buy, or sell goods and services for money

consumers—people who buy goods or services

cricket—a field game similar to baseball that is popular in India

hired—chose a person for a job

products—things that are made or grown to be sold or used

To Learn More

AT THE LIBRARY

Adams, Julia. *101 Awesome Women Who Changed Our World*. London, U.K.: Arcturus Publishing, 2018.

Clinton, Chelsea. *She Persisted Around the World: 13 Women Who Changed History*. New York, N.Y.: Philomel Books, 2018.

Leaf, Christina. *Zaha Hadid*. Minneapolis, Minn.: Bellwether Media, 2019.

ON THE WEB

FACTSURFER

Factsurfer.com gives you a safe, fun way to find more information.

1. Go to www.factsurfer.com.

2. Enter "Indra Nooyi" into the search box.

3. Click the "Surf" button and select your book cover to see a list of related web sites.

Index

The images in this book are reproduced through the courtesy of: PepsiCo, front cover (Indra, product shot), pp. 4-5; Albert Karimov, front cover (factory); focal point, pp. 3, 22 (Pepsi cup); Neville Elder, pp. 6-7; dpa picture alliance, p. 8; Brian Ach, p. 9 (inset); Visual&Written/Newscom, p. 10 (inset); Joe Russo, pp. 10-11; Associated Press, pp. 12-13 (top left); Bill Wippert/Invision/AP, p. 13 (bottom right); Donald Heupel/ Reuters/Newscom, p. 14 (inset); WEF/Photoshot/Newscom, pp. 14-15; Bloomberg, pp. 16-17 (top left); Photoshot/Newscom, p. 17 (bottom right); Spencer Platt, pp. 18-19; Joe Raedle, p. 20 (inset); Paul Morigi, pp. 20-21.